Thomas Jefferson

by Lucia Raatma

Compass Point Early Biographies

Content Adviser: Professor Sherry L. Field,
Department of Social Science Education, College of Education,
The University of Georgia

Reading Adviser: Dr. Linda D. Labbo,
Department of Reading Education, College of Education,
The University of Georgia

COMPASS POINT BOOKS

Minneapolis, Minnesota

Compass Point Books
A Capstone Imprint
151 Good Counsel Drive
P.O. Box 669
Mankato, MN 56002-0669

Visit Compass Point Books on the Internet at *www.capstonepub.com*

Photographs ©:
Stock Montage, cover, 10, 13, 25; Digital Stock, cover; Unicorn Stock Photos/David P. Dill; North Wind Picture
Archives, 5, 16, 22 (top); Hulton Getty/Archive Photos, 6, 9, 18, 19, 20, 24; Archive Photos, 7, 12, 15, 17 (top and
bottom), 22 (bottom), 23; Kent and Donna Dannen, 8; Lambert/Archive Photos, 14; Missouri Historical Society,
St. Louis, 21; Unicorn Stock Photos/C. Schmeiser, 26.

Editors: E. Russell Primm and Emily J. Dolbear
Photo Researcher: Svetlana Zhurkina
Photo Selector: Linda S. Koutris
Designer: Bradfordesign, Inc.

Library of Congress Cataloging-in-Publication Data
Raatma, Lucia.
    Thomas Jefferson / by Lucia Raatma.
        p. cm. — (Compass Point early biographies)
    Includes bibliographical references and index.
    ISBN-13: 978-0-7565-0070-2 (hardcover)
    ISBN-10: 0-7565-0070-2 (hardcover)
    ISBN-13: 978-0-7565-1183-8 (paperback)
    ISBN-10: 0-7565-1183-6 (paperback)
        1. Jefferson, Thomas, 1743–1826—Juvenile literature. 2. Presidents—United States—
Biography—Juvenile literature. [1. Jefferson, Thomas 1743–1826. 2. Presidents.] I. Title. II. Series.
    E332.79 .R3 2001
    973.4'6'092—dc21   00-010939

Table of Contents

The Third President 4

A Young Virginian 5

After College 7

Marriage and Family 9

The Coming Revolution 12

The Second Continental Congress 13

A Public Servant 16

A New Nation 18

The Third President 20

After the White House 22

A Private Citizen 24

The End of a Great Life 27

Important Dates in Thomas Jefferson's Life 28

Glossary 29

Did You Know? 30

Want to Know More? 31

Index 32

The Third President

Thomas Jefferson was the third president of the United States. He was also the main writer of the Declaration of Independence. Thomas Jefferson was one of the Founding Fathers, a group of men who helped make America a new country. He was a very important man in U.S. history.

Thomas Jefferson is pictured on the nickel coin. He is also on the $2 bill, which is not as common as other bills.

Jefferson's picture is on both the nickel and the $2 bill.

A Young Virginian

Thomas Jefferson was born on April 13, 1743, at Shadwell Plantation in Virginia. His father was a wealthy man. He owned a successful **plantation**, a large piece of land on which crops were grown. Thomas's mother came from a respected Virginia family.

Young Thomas was well educated. For a time, he studied with a private teacher. Later he attended fine schools in Virginia.

Thomas attended a school like this one.

When he was seventeen, he went to the College of William and Mary in Williamsburg, Virginia.

After College

After two years of college, Thomas left to study law. He studied with George Wythe, a friend of one of his teachers. There were no law schools at this time.

George Wythe

Thomas studied and worked with Mr. Wythe for five years. Then Thomas became a lawyer himself.

◄ Thomas went to the College of William and Mary when he was seventeen years old.

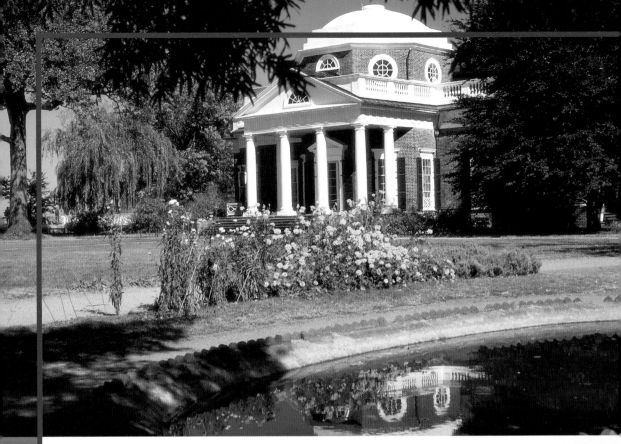

Jefferson designed his home at Monticello.

While he practiced law, Thomas also worked on his plantation in Virginia. It was called Monticello. He got the land for it when his father died. Jefferson designed the home that was built on the plantation.

Marriage and Family

In 1772, a few months before he turned twenty-nine, Thomas got married. His wife was Martha Wayles Skelton.

Both Martha and Thomas enjoyed music. She played the piano and the **harpsichord**. A harpsichord looks like a piano but has two keyboards. Martha and Thomas Jefferson had

Thomas married Martha Wayles Skelton in 1772.

9

a happy marriage. But Martha was often sick. They had six children. Only two daughters lived to be adults. Martha Jefferson died in 1782. Thomas and Martha had been married only ten years.

For several years, Thomas Jefferson was a member of the Virginia **House of Burgesses**. He held a number of local offices. Soon he began to work on a bigger project.

◀ Jefferson's daughter, Martha Jefferson Randolph

The Coming Revolution

At this time, the United States was not yet a country. It was a group of **colonies** that was governed by England.

Many Americans did not want to be controlled by another country. They wanted freedom. These feelings in the colonies led to the American Revolution. This was the war against England for America's freedom.

Bunker Hill was a key battle in the American Revolution.

The Second Continental Congress

During the American Revolution, Thomas was elected to the Second Continental Congress. He was asked by that group to write the Declaration of Independence. He was a very good writer and was very smart as well.

The Declaration of Independence told

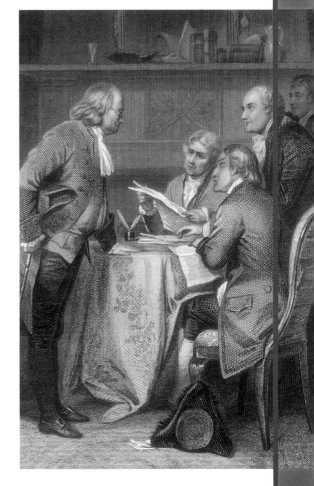

Thomas Jefferson (second from left) was the main writer of the Declaration of Independence.

13

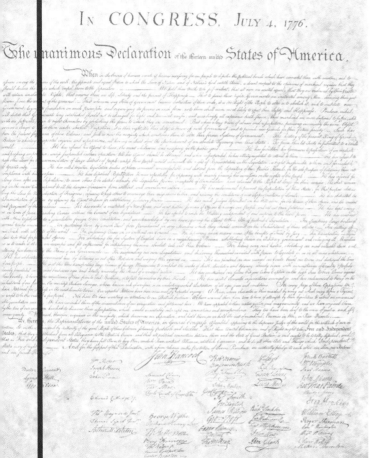

The Declaration of Independence

England that the colonies wanted freedom. The document said that all people were equal. It also said that people should control their own government. The creation of the United States of America was based on these ideas.

Other men helped write the Declaration

of Independence. But most of the words were Thomas's. On July 4, 1776, the document was **adopted**. The United States remembers this day as Independence Day.

The signing of the Declaration of Independence

A Public Servant

Thomas continued to serve the public. He
worked to make the government better. He
tried to make fairer laws for owning land.
For many years, only rich people owned land.
Only men who owned land could vote.

Thomas also worked hard for religious

freedom. He believed
that the government
could not control a
person's beliefs. He also
made sure that religious
groups could not control
the government.

Jefferson believed in religious freedom. The Pilgrims
first came to North America for this freedom.

Benjamin Franklin

Thomas Jefferson was governor of Virginia for two years. He was also the United States **minister** to France. There he worked with other ministers. Other U.S. ministers working in France included Benjamin Franklin and John Adams. Thomas Jefferson enjoyed his time in France. He learned much about the French people.

John Adams

A New Nation

After the American Revolution, George Washington was made the first president of the United States. President Washington asked Thomas Jefferson to be his secretary of state in 1790. Thomas Jefferson was only forty-seven years old.

Later, John Adams was elected the second president of the United States. Thomas Jefferson was his vice president. And then, in 1800, Thomas Jefferson was elected to be the third president of the United States.

Thomas Jefferson was the third president of the United States.

◀ George Washington, Thomas Jefferson, and Alexander Hamilton, the first secretary of the treasury

The Third President

As president, Thomas Jefferson did a great deal for the country. He made the Louisiana Purchase. This act gave the new country a very large piece of land. Thomas Jefferson also sent Meriwether Lewis and William Clark on their travels. Lewis and Clark explored much of what is now the American West.

The Louisiana Purchase added a vast amount of land to the United States.

Lewis and Clark explored the new land for President Jefferson. ➤

Thomas Jefferson was elected president a second time. During his second term, there was war in Europe. France and England were fighting over trading rights. Thomas Jefferson worked hard to keep the United States out of the war.

After the White House

Some people wanted Thomas Jefferson to be president a third time. But he wanted to go home to Monticello.

Jefferson returning home to Monticello

Thomas Jefferson returned home in 1808. He enjoyed working with plants. He also made changes to his home. He invented many things. He created the swivel chair and an improved plow. He also enjoyed experiment-ing with clocks and engines.

Jefferson designed this writing desk. ➤

Jefferson sold many of his books to the Library of Congress.

Thomas Jefferson also spent much time reading and collecting books. He liked history, religion, law, and many other subjects.

The original Library of Congress in Washington had burned in 1814. Thomas Jefferson sold the new library 6,500 books from his collection. These books rebuilt the Library of Congress.

A Private Citizen

Thomas Jefferson continued to do important work as an older man. He founded the University of Virginia when he was seventy-six years old. He decided on the best place for the school. He designed both the buildings and the grounds. And he even helped plan the first classes at the new university.

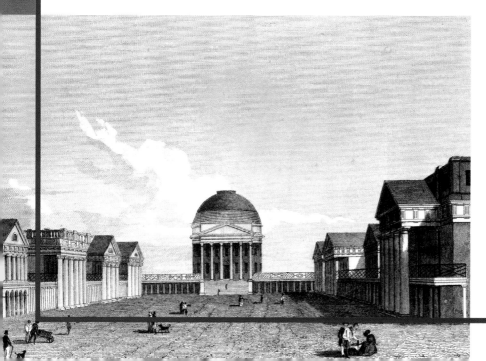

Jefferson founded the University of Virginia. He also designed many of its buildings.

Jefferson tried to end the owning of slaves.

Throughout his life, Thomas Jefferson had slaves on his plantations. Because they were property, they did not get paid for their work. Slavery was widespread in the South. Thomas Jefferson was never happy about slavery. He tried many times to end slavery. But he was never successful. Slavery was an issue for the United States for many years to come. Arguments about slavery finally led to the Civil War.

The End of a Great Life

Thomas Jefferson died on July 4, 1826. That was the fiftieth anniversary of the signing of the Declaration of Independence. Thomas Jefferson was eighty-three years old. He was buried at Monticello. Thomas Jefferson is remembered as a fine writer and an important thinker. His ideas helped create the United States of America.

◀ Jefferson's grave

Important Dates in Thomas Jefferson's Life

1743	Born on April 13 in Virginia
1769–1775	Serves in the Virginia House of Burgesses
1772	Marries Martha Wayles Skelton
1775–1776	Serves in the Second Continental Congress
1776	Writes and signs the Declaration of Independence and serves in the Virginia General Assembly
1779	Is elected governor of Virginia
1784–1789	Serves as U.S. minister to France
1790–1793	Serves as secretary of state under George Washington
1793–1801	Serves as vice president under John Adams
1801–1809	Is president of the United States
1819	Founds the University of Virginia
1826	Dies on July 4 at Monticello in Virginia

Glossary

adopted— approved

colonies—political areas that are controlled by another country

harpsichord—a musical instrument with two keyboards

House of Burgesses—the part of Virginia's colonial government that created laws

minister—a person who represents his or her country's government in another country

plantation—a large piece of land on which crops were grown

Did You Know?

- Thomas Jefferson was skilled at many things. He was an architect, an inventor, a scientist, a lawyer, and a farmer.

- With the Louisiana Purchase, Thomas Jefferson more than doubled the size of the United States.

- Thomas Jefferson and John Adams, the second president of the United States, died on the same day—July 4, 1826.

Want to Know More?

At the Library

Adler, David A. *A Picture Book of Thomas Jefferson.* New York: Holiday House, 1990.

Usel, T. M. *Thomas Jefferson: A Photo-Illustrated Biography.* Mankato, Minn.: Bridgestone Books, 1996.

On the Web

For more information on *Thomas Jefferson,* use FactHound to track down Web sites related to this book.

1. Go to *http://www.compasspointbooks.com/facthound*
2. Type in this book ID: 0756500702
3. Click on the *Fetch It* button.

Your trusty FactHound will fetch the best Web sites for you!

Through the Mail

Thomas Jefferson Memorial
900 Ohio Drive, S.W.
Washington, DC 20024-2000
To visit the memorial in the capital city

On the Road

Monticello
Charlottesville, VA 22902
804/984-9822
To tour Thomas Jefferson's house

Index

Adams, John, 17, *17*, 19
American Revolution, 12–13
Battle of Bunker Hill, *12*
birth, 5
Civil War, 25
Clark, William, 20, *21*
College of William and Mary, 6, *6*
colonies, 12, 29
death, 26, 27
Declaration of Independence, 4, 13–15, *14*, *15*, 27
education, 5–7, *5*
Founding Fathers, 4
France, 17
Franklin, Benjamin, 17, *17*
Hamilton, Alexander, 18
harpsichord, 9, 29
House of Burgesses, 11, 29
Independence Day, 15
inventions, 22, *22*
Jefferson, Martha Wayles, 9, *9*
Jefferson, Thomas, 4, *13*, 18, *19*, 22
land ownership, 16

Lewis, Meriwether, 20, *21*
Library of Congress, 23, *23*
Louisiana Purchase, 20, *20*
map, *20*
marriage, 9
ministers, 17, 29
money, 4, *4*
Monticello, 8, *8*, 22, *22*, 27
Pilgrims, *16*
plantations, 5, 8, 29
president, 19, 21
Randolph, Martha Jefferson, *10*, 11
religious freedom, 16, *16*
Second Continental Congress, 13
secretary of state, 18
Shadwell Plantation, 5
slavery, 25, *25*
University of Virginia, 24, *24*
vice president, 19
Washington, George, 18
writing desk, 22
Wythe, George, 7, *7*

About the Author

Lucia Raatma received her bachelor's degree in English literature from the University of South Carolina and her master's degree in cinema studies from New York University. She has written a wide range of books for young people. When she is not researching or writing, she enjoys going to movies, playing tennis, and spending time with her husband, daughter, and golden retriever.